ALASKAN PROPS

ALASKAN PROPS

KARL-HEINZ MORAWIETZ & JÖRG WEIER

Osprey Colour Series

Published in 1988 by Osprey Publishing Limited
27A Floral Street, London WC2E 9DP
Member company of the George Philip Group

British Library Cataloguing in Publication Data

Morawietz, Karl-Heinz
    Alaskan props.—(Osprey colour series)
    1. Alaska. Commercial propeller-driven aeroplanes,
    1940–1960
    I. Title   II. Weier, Jörg
    629.133′343

ISBN 0-85045-869-2

Editor Dennis Baldry
Captions by Mike Jerram
Designed by David Tarbutt
Printed in Hong Kong

Title pages Still showing signs of its former life
in the United States Air Force, N1036F came off
Douglas's Santa Monica production line in 1952
as C-118A Liftmaster 51-3834

Front cover Resident in Alaska since 1964,
Curtiss C-46 Commando N1663M is currently
registered to John O'Magoffin but retains the
patriotic blue and gold livery of the now defunct
Interior Airways. The snow covered peaks of the
Chugach Mountains can be seen in the
background

Back cover One of Northern Air Cargo's
immaculate fleet of Douglas DC-6s glistens on
the Anchorage ramp

Contents

Terminal building, Aleutian style. Not much by Heathrow, JFK or O'Hare standards, but Reeve Aleutian's quonset hut provides a warm welcome for travellers at Cold Bay, Alaska

Northern Air Cargo

Chilly external preflight completed, Northern Air Cargo skipper Captain Mark Culver (right) gets ready to saddle up Three Six Fox for a flight to King Salmon on the Alaskan peninsula

En route. Three Six Fox's wingtip points to the 6509 feet summit of Black Peak Mountain

Yes, it really is Three Six Fox, faded Military Airlift Command paint replaced by fresh Northern Air Cargo colours for the 1985 season as she taxies away from the Anchorage ramp

Overleaf Northern Lights. Internal and external illumination, the C-118A gets attention to its No 4 2500 hp Pratt & Whitney R2800-52W

Three Northern Air Cargo DC-6As lined up on the Anchorage ramp in the sunshine of an Alaskan morning in 1986. NAC bought its first DC-6 in 1969, and has subsequently increased the fleet to a round dozen

Like sister ship Three Six Fox, N1027N is a former USAF C-118A acquired from the Military Aircraft Storage and Disposition Centre (MASDC) 'boneyard' at Davis-Monthan AFB, Arizona

Overleaf Typically flatulent start from Two Seven November's Double Wasps on another quick turn around during Alaska's short summer season. Northern Air Cargo flies scheduled services to 23 communities within Alaska, keeping the reliable 'Dizzy Sixes' active 24 hours a day

Inset Two Seven November taxies against a threatening backdrop of 'stuffed cloud' — Alaska's Chugach mountain range

15

Upward opening fore and aft freight doors were a standard feature of the DC-6A, whose reinforced cabin floor can take up to 28,188 lbs of cargo

Ground power carts are close companions of the aircraft on Northern Air Cargo's ramp because . . .

. . . time is money and as soon as the last piece of cargo is secured and N313RS has taken on a load of 100 octane, she's off the blocks and bound for Kodiak Island, an hour and a half's flying time away

The virginal white DC-6A N7780B was built for cargo carrier Riddle, but was once owned by multi-millionaire recluse Howard Hughes, perhaps accounting for its incredibly low total of only nine hours fifty minutes logged when Northern Air Cargo bought it in 1973

Cargo netted, paperwork complete and doors secured, NAC's Captain Doug Lee fires up Eighty Bravo's 10,000 horses, and is quick to get the gear up and the Six accelerating as he departs from Anchorage

NORTHERN AIR CARGO

RESTRICTED AREA
AUTHORIZED VEHICLES
ONLY

Stage struck. This beautiful nose art was painted on N99330's *aloominum* canvas by a talented young lady from Tucson, but sadly will not be retained when the travel weary DC-6A/C goes into service with Northern Air Cargo. The aircraft was bought from Carnegie Holdings of Edmonton, Canada in 1987, and has been around a bit, as the flags of all nations attest

N7919C is Northern Air Cargo's sole tanker aircraft, capable of carrying up to 4500 US gallons of fuel. Once a passenger carrying airliner with Reeve Aleutian Airways, '19C has lived in Alaska for 33 years. During the 1983 season the aircraft operated out of Fairbanks, running fuel supplies to the Dall Creek gold mine in a remote area close to the Polar Circle

N7919C's First Officer 'Smitty' Smith holds her steady while Flight Engineer Marty Loeblein attends to the paperwork, not a uniform jacket or gold stripe to be seen. Nor a CRT display or sidestick controller, just big round analog instruments and man-sized control wheels, throttles and mixture levers

Badly mangled remains of a Fairchild C-119
bulldozed to the side of the gravel strip provide
a stark reminder that Alaskan flying is never
easy, no matter how experienced the pilot

Left Framed by the nosegear of a sister ship, Two Seven November's cargo doors gape open awaiting another load

Above and above left Big friend, slightly smaller friend. A Flying Tigers' Boeing 747-200F towers over Northern Air Cargo's bulk tanker on the cargo ramp. The all-freight Jumbos' cargo capacity is almost double the maximum take-off weight of a DC-6A, but don't try putting one into a short airstrip

Open air maintenance is SOP in the hectic short Alaskan summer to keep downtime to the minimum. Here the decowled 2500 hp Double Wasp CB17s of DC-6A N4206L get a dose of tender loving care from a NAC powerplant expert

Despite having seen thirty or more summers (and harsh winters) Northern Air Cargo's Douglasses are in sparkling condition, as (literally) reflected by the polished skin of DC-6A N1377K

Overleaf Seventy Seven Kilo taxies across the Anchorage ramp against the dominant presence of the Chugach Mountains

Washing machines, motorcycles, fragile
glassware, all part of a NAC DC-6A's daily
round. The old Sixes may even rival Maytags
for dependability and long service

Preceding pages and right Seen in snow and sunshine, N6813C was built for, but never delivered to, the British independent carrier Airwork. Her first operator was Slick Airways, and she became Northern Air Cargo's first DC-6A in 1969. One Three Charlie was christened *Taiwan Clipper* after crossing the Pacific to Taiwan for a major overhaul. Vintage Chevrolet truck's wing appears to have had a recent argument with something

Two a-turnin' (and another pair on the other side) as N6818C begins the descent into Kodiak Island

N434TA joined Northern Air Cargo in 1987 after
12 years with Detroit-based freight carrier
Zantop

Surplus military Fairchild C-82 twin boom
transports like N4752C helped Northern Air
Cargo get established in Alaska. None of NAC's
C-82s still flies

Markair

Formerly known as Alaska International Air,
Markair operates a mixed fleet of Boeing 737
and Lockheed L-100 Hercules on scheduled
passenger and cargo services throughout
Alaska and to Seattle, Washington. Here L-100-
30 N107AK is prepared for departure from
Anchorage International to Unalakleet via Nome
on the evening of 15 July 1986

N107AK's crew spotted these bush fires en route to Nome. Ground staff there unloaded the big freighter in less than 20 minutes—quite long enough at that chilly and inhospitable location near the Polar Circle

Sun screens and Ray-Bans are needed as characteristic Alaskan late evening light floods the spacious flight deck through the L-100's 15 cockpit windows

After a short hop over Norton Sound the unladen Herc set down on Unalakleet's gravel runway to take on a payload of fish bound for Anchorage

Lower left On top of the world. Well, quite close. N107AK's flight engineer invited co-author Karl-Heinz Morawietz to take the Alaskan air from the L-100's 'roof garden'

Lockheed has sold 109 L-100 civil freighter
versions of the ubiquitous C-130 Hercules

Land of the midnight sun. N107AK at 20,000 feet,
departing from Unalakleet just after the witching
hour. On a few summer days in the Alaskan
north the sun shines right around the clock

Same aircraft, different outfit. Markair's L-100s share airspace with military Hercules like this Alaska Air National Guard C-130E of the 176th TAC Airlift Group at Kulis ANG base, Anchorage International Airport

Markair has three of these L-100-30 stretched versions of the commercial Hercules, which have a maximum payload of 51,054 lbs

New name, old colours. When operated by
Alaska International N108AK was a familiar
visitor to European airports, but Markair confine
their operations to Alaska and the US mainland

Northern Pacific Transport

Few Alaskan load haulers wear such bright—if heavily weathered—colours as this Ball Brothers C-47. Founded by Gerald C Ball, and renamed Northern Pacific Transport in 1982, the company is one of the longest established cargo carriers in Alaska. It operates a mixed fleet of mostly MASDC-surplus Douglas C-47s, C-118s and Fairchild C-82 and C-119 Packets, hauling general cargo and fish

Resting in winter alongside another, engineless, example of her breed, C-119 Packet N8504X gets attention from Northern Pacific Transport maintenance staff at NPT's Anchorage base, while a Northwest Airlines Boeing 747 launches disdainfully into the murk. Derived from the C-82 (illustrated in Chapter 1) the C-119 'Flying

Boxcar' first flew in 1947 and was built by Fairchild and Kaiser Industries, remaining in production until October 1955, when the 1112th aircraft was delivered to the USAF. The C-119 served in the Korean and Vietnam wars. Fifty-two were modified as AC-119G Shadow and AC-199K Stinger gunships for 'Spooky' operations in Vietnam

Looking for oil leaks is par for the course when your aeroplanes fly on big round engines

A thorough ground check of the Boxcar's 3500 hp Wright R-3350-89 Cyclone engines is vital before return to service. Never blessed with excess performance at high gross weights, the C-119 is unflatteringly known as the 'flying coffin' among Boxcar old timers. This one has a podded Westinghouse J34 jet engine to boost take-off and climb performance—a common add-on to commercially operated Packets

Preceding pages Gasoline alley. N9027X, a stock C-119G without jet boost, awaits an afternoon trip to collect salmon from Egegik, where it lands right on the sandy beach. Now that's what you call freshly flown-in fish . . .

N12347, one of NPT's DC-6As, was built at Santa Monica in 1953 for the Flying Tiger Line. Leased to Northwest Airlines until 1961, she subsequently flew with Zantop, Southern Airways and TAISA of Costa Rica before returning to the USA in 1975 for service as a fire bomber with Sis-Q Flying Services in California. The versatile Six made the 'Last Frontier' state her home in 1980

It's an, er, um . . . Don't fret if you cannot put a name to this rare and portly Alaskan bird, for it is the only surviving example of Virginius E Clark's nine-seat Pilgrim 100, built by the American Airplane & Engine Corporation at Farmingdale on Long Island in 1931–32. Sixteen Pratt & Whitney Hornet-engined Pilgrim 100As and six Wright Cyclone-engined 100Bs were originally operated by American Airlines, later passing to Alaskan Airways and Pan American's Pacific-Alaska division. The Pilgrim's tubby profile stems from its under floor baggage and cargo compartments. After a working life spanning half a century Northern Pacific Transport's pristine N709Y has attained rare antique status, and no longer flies

The smaller companies

In the months of June and July millions of salmon return from the open sea to spawn in Alaskan waters. It is a lucrative time for fishermen, and for the cargo companies who ferry their catch from small airfields along the coastline to the fish processing plants at Anchorage and Kodiak Island. Here former USAF C-97G Stratofreighter N297HP operated by Hawkins & Powers of Greybull, Wyoming, waits at King Salmon Airport for a full load trip back to Anchorage

Flying fish. The C-97G's temperamental, maintenance-hog and occasionally pyrotechnic 3500 hp Pratt & Whitney R-4360-59 Wasp Majors thrumming along on top on 9 July 1983 when N297HP made three return flights between Anchorage International and King Salmon

Captain Gene Powers, co-owner of Hawkins &
Powers, is a true 'hands on' boss, seen here in
the left seat of the Stratofreighter

Jeppesen approach plate for King Salmon
Airport clipped to the glareshield, Powers, flying
his third salmon run of the day, eyes the
weather through the C-97G's glasshouse

Hawkins & Powers based two C-97Gs at Anchorage for the 1983 salmon season, operating on behalf of the Whitney Fidalgo Fish Company

Not too many Curtiss C-46 Commandos still fly in the far north. Fairbanks-based Cliff Everts bought this snow-encrusted example from the Japanese Air Self-Defense Force, whose faded dayglo trim it still bore when photographed at Anchorage International in the winter of 1982

The C-46's cockpit was the original 'flying greenhouse'. From its multi-faceted windows a 'Dumbo' pilot can (in one respect at least) look down on drivers of more modern machinery such as Boeing 727s. Note half moon controls and massive trim wheels. Mmmmm . . . you can almost smell the sweat-stained leather, oil, avgas, hydraulic fluid and stale stodgy smoke. Pure nostalgia. If you could bottle it, you'd make a fortune among Big Props buffs

Trade you for a Learjet? Not likely. Fairbanks-Metro Field-based Air North maintained this 1938 DC-3A-197B in executive configuration, with pleasingly contemporary interior furnishings. NC18944 was built at Santa Monica and delivered to United Airlines on 27 April 1938 as *Mainliner Omaha*, later becoming *Mainliner Bend*. It logged 50,846 flight hours before retiring from United service in May 1954. No longer operated by Air North, it was last heard of in storage at Guatemala City

Air North painted each of its DC-3s in a different livery. N3FY, in a mostly natural metal scheme reminiscent of the type's airline heyday in the United States, bears the appropriate title *Grand Old Lady* and a nice line in grandma artwork

Pictured at Fairbanks-Metro Airport in July 1983, Air North DC-3 N8042X has since been sold to another Alaskan carrier, Audi Air

Faded paintwork reveals that this time worn DC-3 was once on the Federal Aviation Administration's navaid checking fleet, its FAA seal hastily replaced by the 'logo' of Winky's Fish—The Flying Circus. William 'Winky' Crawford began hauling fish in Alaska in 1983, and has since upgraded to a Lockheed 1049 Super Constellation

Until it ceased operations on 18 January 1986, Seeair Alaska provided passenger services between Anchorage and communities such as Aniak, Bethel and St Mary's, using DHC-6 Twin Otter and Convair CV-580 turboprops, including N5822

Right All cowlings off Pacific Star Seafood Company Inc's C-54 Skymaster N898AL as ground crew prepare her 1540 hp Pratt & Whitney R-2800s for the 1983 fishing season

Overleaf Aviation Traders Limited of Southern, England engineered the unlovely but practical ATL-98 Carvair conversion of the Douglas DC-4 in 1961. The bulbous nose section with raised flight deck enabled cars to be driven aboard through its hydraulically operated, sideways-opening nose door. The Carvair also incorporated DC-6 brakes and the DC-7's larger fin and rudder to compensate for the additional keel area up front. This one, formerly British Air Ferries' *Porky Pete*, arrived in the USA in 1979, but made only a few flights into Alaska during 1982 while operated by the now defunct Gifford Aviation

Stebbins & Ambler

A perfect example of self-help, 'Alaska's first native air transport company' was formed by the villages of Stebbins and Ambler to keep themselves supplied with vital goods

Stebbins & Ambler's fleet comprises just one aircraft, this Fairchild C-119 Packet, with two other grounded Boxcars cannibalized for spares to keep N1394N flying

106

There's only one flight crew too, made up of pilot Jim Devine, copilot Bob Jaidinger and engineer John Reffett, so it is a case of 'all hands to the pump' when topping off N1394N's fuel tanks. After years of battling through weather the old Boxcar's wing leading edges look as if they've been attacked with a ball-peen hammer

Shot from the navigator's astrodome and neatly framed by VHF antennae is the C-119's dorsally-mounted Stewart-Davis jet booster pack—a podded 3800 lb st Westinghouse J34 turbojet engine which provides enhanced take-off and climb performance and greater safety margins when operating from short runways in mountainous terrain

N1394N's 3500 hp Wright R-3500s are run up under critical eyes prior to the start of a trip over the high peaks of the Chigmit mountain range to Manokotak, 300 miles south east of Anchorage on Nushagak Bay. Stebbins & Ambler are restricted to VFR operations, so destination and alternate airports and en route weather must be within VMC limits. This flight was delayed for two days awaiting VFR conditions

En route passing through the Chigmits. Climbing fast is not the old Boxcar's forté. As flight engineer John Reffett puts it: 'Before we reach 12,000 feet altitude we're in Japan.' Nice one!

With sun blinds drawn and styrofoam cup of coffee to hand, Devine and crew may seem relaxed, but steering a visual path through a mountain range using the Mark 1 eyeball to compare ground features with maps demands a very high level of concentration even when you are familiar with the terrain

After a two hour flight the Stebbins & Ambler crew were on short finals to Manokotak's narrow, 2600 ft gravel airstrip (upper left of the picture) when a truck pulled onto the runway, necessitating a late go-around

No trucks on the second approach, and with
maximum reverse thrust the C-119 came to a
halt within feet of the strip's end. Harsh reverse
pitch caused three litres of hydraulic fluid to
escape through the propellers' dome seals.
When the crew had replenished vital fluids they
faced the additional chore of unloading the
Boxcar with no outside help save for a pair of
C-119 buffs/photographers

Left The perfect airport? Uncluttered airspace, little traffic, never heard of noise abatement procedures or protesting environmentalists

'Ready to rock'n'roll!' calls Captain Jim Devine and copilot Bob Jaidinger hangs onto a windscreen brace as the C-119, Wrights turning and J34 burning, starts its take-off run down Manokotak's strip. Devine says he *has* flown in and out of shorter runways, but not again, thank you very much

Perfect VFR weather and an eye-level view of Alaska's spectacular landscape made for a memorable return trip to Anchorage

Reeve Aleutian

Bob Reeve is one of Alaska's most celebrated aviation pioneers. A former barnstormer and mail pilot for Pan American-Grace Airways in South America, Reeve arrived in Valdez in 1932 with $2 in his pocket, rebuilt a wrecked Eaglerock biplane and began carrying gold prospectors to stake their claims on tiny offshore islands. Today Reeve Aleutian operates a fleet of modern turboprop and jet aircraft on scheduled services throughout the Aleutian Islands chain, including a direct flight from Cold Bay on the tip of the Alaskan peninsula to

Seattle, Washington. Here one of Reeve's three Japanese-built mixed passenger/cargo NAMC YS-11 twin turboprops is seen on the ramp at Anchorage International on a summer's evening in 1983

Overleaf inset Although its airline career in the 'Lower 48' was marred by early crashes, the Lockheed L-188 Electra continues to give good service in South America and in Alaska, where Reeve Aleutian's N178RV is seen being towed to the apron at Anchorage from the airline's maintenance base

Overleaf Electra N1968R is a true survivor in best Alaskan style. En route from Cold Bay to Seattle in June 1983 the paddle bladed propeller of its No 2 4050 shp Allison 501D-15 turboprop broke away, cutting into the fuselage and destroying control linkages. With only cruise power and very limited directional control available, the crew managed to return to Anchorage where Reeve's skilled engineers rebuilt the aircraft and returned it to service

Last page A passenger's eye view of the Electra's humming Allison turboprops